DODD, MEAD WONDERS BOOKS include WONDERS OF:

ALLIGATORS AND CROCODILES.
  Blassingame
ANIMAL NURSERIES. Berrill
BARNACLES. Ross and Emerson
BAT WORLD. Lavine
BEYOND THE SOLAR SYSTEM.
  Feravolo
BISON WORLD. Lavine and Scuro
CACTUS WORLD. Lavine
CAMELS. Lavine
CARIBOU. Rearden
CATTLE. Scuro
CORALS AND CORAL REEFS.
  Jacobson and Franz
CROWS. Blassingame
DINOSAUR WORLD. Matthews
DONKEYS. Lavine and Scuro
DUST. McFall
EAGLE WORLD. Lavine
ELEPHANTS. Lavine and Scuro
FLY WORLD. Lavine
FROGS AND TOADS. Blassingame
GEESE AND SWANS. Fegely
GEMS. Pearl
GOATS. Lavine and Scuro
GRAVITY. Feravolo
HAWK WORLD. Lavine
HERBS. Lavine
HOW ANIMALS LEARN. Berrill
HUMMINGBIRDS. Simon
JELLYFISH. Jacobson and Franz
KELP FOREST. Brown
LLAMAS. Perry
LIONS. Schaller
MARSUPIALS. Lavine

MEASUREMENT. Lieberg
MICE. Lavine
MONKEY WORLD. Berrill
MOSQUITO WORLD. Ault
OWL WORLD. Lavine
PELICAN WORLD. Cook and Schreiber
PONIES. Lavine and Casey
PRAIRIE DOGS. Chace
PRONGHORN. Chace
RACCOONS. Blassingame
RATTLESNAKES. Chace
ROCKS AND MINERALS. Pearl
SEA GULLS. Schreiber
SEA HORSES. Brown
SEALS AND SEA LIONS. Brown
SNAILS AND SLUGS. Jacobson and
  Franz
SPIDER WORLD. Lavine
SPONGES. Jacobson and Pang
STARFISH. Jacobson and Emerson
STORKS. Kahl
TERNS. Schreiber
TERRARIUMS. Lavine
TREE WORLD. Cosgrove
TURTLE WORLD. Blassingame
WILD DUCKS. Fegely
WOODS AND DESERT AT NIGHT. Berrill
WORLD OF THE ALBATROSS. Fisher
WORLD OF BEARS. Bailey
WORLD OF HORSES. Lavine and Casey
WORLD OF SHELLS. Jacobson and
  Emerson
WORLD OF WOLVES. Berrill
YOUR SENSES. Cosgrove

WONDERS OF

MICE

Sigmund A. Lavine

Illustrated with photographs and old prints

DODD, MEAD & COMPANY · NEW YORK

For Herb—
  only because of Miriam

Illustrations courtesy of: Bing and Grøndahl, 21; Chilmark Pewter Sculpture by Lance International, 44; A. Epstein, Boston Ballet Company, 31; Field Museum of Natural History, Chicago, 40, 62, 65, 66; Robert Foley, 22, 23; Scotty Getchell, Battelle Laboratories, 46 *bottom*; Lloyd Ingles, 52, 59; The Jackson Laboratory, Bar Harbor, Me., 18, 74, 75, 77; Knickerbocker Toys (c) Walt Disney Productions, 29; Lunt Galleries, Greenfield, Ma., 30; Richard McCarty, University of Virginia, 50; Jane O'Regan, 8, 9, 10, 11, 12, 13, 19, 56; Edwin Way Teale, 68; U. S. Fish and Wildlife Service, 43, 46 *top*; Alex Walker, 70; Peter Weber, 6, 27, 32, 34, 35, 37; Zoological Society of London, 14, 57, 78.

1 2 3 4 5 6 7 8 9 10

Library of Congress Cataloging in Publication Data

Lavine, Sigmund A
  Wonders of mice.

  Includes index.
  1. Mice—Juvenile literature. I. Title.
QL737.R638L38   599.32′33   80–1018
ISBN 0–396–07891–5

CONTENTS

1 Meet the Mice   7
   Family History   10
   Mice Old and New   12
2 Mouse Lore   16
3 House Mice   33
4 Field Mice   41
5 Hunters and Harvesters   47
   Grasshopper Mice   47
   Harvest Mice   51
   Pocket Mice   56
6 Fascinating Mice   61
   Jumping Mice   62
   Deer Mice   64
   Climbing Mice   69
7 Laboratory Mice   73
   Index   79

Framed by weather-beaten boards, a house mouse poses for its picture.

1. Meet the Mice

"In numbers as sand and dust"—Homer

Man has always despised mice. Some of this dislike stems from the ancient belief that mice are creatures of evil in league with the Devil. There are also logical reasons for man's attitude toward mice. Although small in size, mice are responsible for tremendous economic loss every year. They destroy standing crops, consume and contaminate huge amounts of stored foodstuffs, and, while gathering nesting materials, ruin yards of fabric and tons of paper. In addition, mice are carriers of a number of diseases.

Because mice do so much damage and spread germs, we are apt to forget that certain species of mice are beneficial. These friends of man eat untold millions of destructive insects annually. Moreover, the mouse (in its albino form) plays a vital role in scientific research.

Zoologists—students of animal life—have identified hundreds of species of mice. Other undiscovered species probably live throughout the world. All mice are gnawing animals. Therefore they are members of the order Rodentia. Scientists derived the word Rodentia—shortened to rodents in common speech—from the Latin *radere* (to gnaw).

Over half the total living species of mammals are rodents. The mice comprise one of the largest groups in this vast horde. Indeed, it is impossible to estimate accurately the world's mouse population.

Like all rodents, mice have a physical characteristic that distinguishes them from all other mammals—sixteen teeth adapted for gnawing and nibbling. While most mammals have four canines (long, pointed teeth designed for tearing or stabbing), rodents lack these. Instead, there is a pair of large chisel-like teeth (incisors) in the front of each jaw. The jaws also contain three molars on each side used for grinding. A wide gap separates the four incisors from the grinders, which are located far back in the mouth. Rodents' teeth are most efficient tools. Thus it is impossible to confine a pet mouse to a wooden or wire cage.

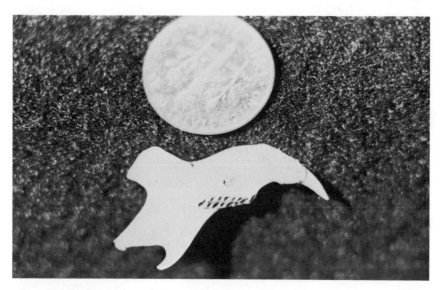

This jaw of a house mouse was taken from an owl pellet (undigested regurgitated material). The compound molars have fallen out, but characteristic multiple socket is diagnostic. The dime is for scale.

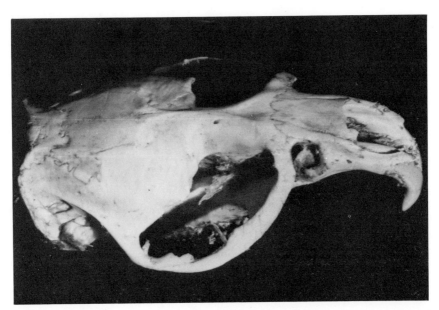

Two views of a Norway rat skull, from above and below, showing typical rodent dentition. Note the compound molars which characterize these Old World rodents.

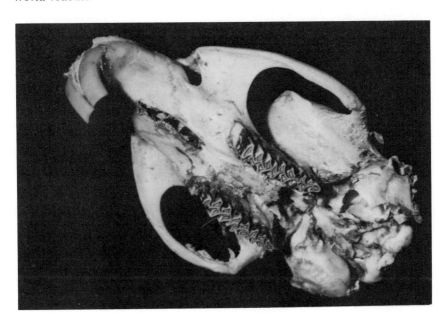

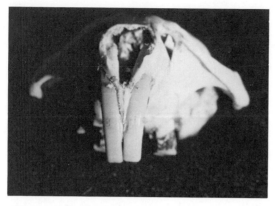

Photo of skull of Norway rat showing incisors; drawing by Jane O'Regan from beneath rodent showing incisors

Because rodents gnaw constantly, it would appear that sooner or later the incisors should grind down to mere stubs. But not only do the incisors never stop growing, they also remain sharp. This is because the hard enamel that covers the front of the incisors wears more slowly than the soft bone that makes up the rest of the tooth.

If an incisor is damaged, rodents cannot feed properly. The cutting teeth are so located that they work against each other like scissors blades. When one breaks off, growth of the opposite incisor is unchecked. The tooth may even grow into a long, curved tusk. Usually, however, a rodent dies of starvation if one of its "chisels" is injured.

Family History

For convenience, scientists have divided the Rodentia into three large groups: Sciuromorphs (squirrel like), Hystricomorphs (porcupine like), and the Myomorphs (mouse like). The last category not only does the most damage but also it surpasses the other two groups both in species and in numbers.

Fossils reveal that the ancestor of the Myomorphs was a tree-dwelling creature equipped with claws for climbing, a long tail for balancing, and extremely sharp teeth. Both rats and mice probably originated in Asia during the Oligocene period some forty million years ago. As the centuries passed, their descendants reached Africa, the Orient, and South America. In all these areas, numerous new species developed from the original stock. Incidentally, in former times no distinction was made between "rat" and "mouse," and "mouse" was employed to identify both animals. Today, popular usage determines whether a specific rodent is called a mouse or a rat. Generally speaking, "mouse" is used to identify small specimens, "rat" to describe larger ones.

The rodents that comprise the Myomorphs differ greatly in size, habits, and habitat. Among them are the economically important muskrat, destructive rats, dormice noted for long hibernations, emigrating lemmings, and the gerbils and hamsters raised by hobbyists. Other Myomorphs are not so well known to laymen. As a matter of fact, even specialists find it difficult to distinguish between certain species.

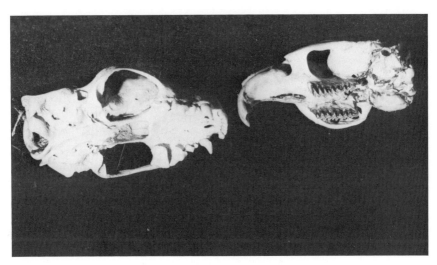

Photo shows comparative size of skulls of cat, left, and Norway rat.

Actually, the only Myomorphs that are closely related are two conglomerations of mice, rats, and voles which are known to zoologists as the Cricetids and the Murids. It is estimated that there are about two thousand species of Cricetids while there are so many species and subspecies of Murids that it is quite impossible to enumerate them correctly. One thing is certain—there are so many Murids that they make up about a third of all known mammals.

Scientists have labeled the Cricetids "ancient mice." This is because their ancestry can be traced back to the mice of the Oligocene period. The Murids did not appear until a much later time. Therefore they are called "modern mice."

By the time the Murids developed, the Cricetids were well established. But they could not compete with the newcomers, who rapidly extended their range, forcing the Cricetids to find homes far to the south. However, although the Murids spread far and wide, no member of the group reached the New World until man accidentally gave the brown and black rats and the house mouse free passage across the Atlantic.

Mice Old and New

Instead of employing the technical terms "ancient mice" and "modern mice," this book identifies all the mice described as either Old World or New World species. Wherever the word mouse appears, it is used in its popular sense—a small rodent

 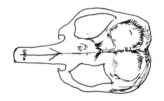

Drawings of skulls of a house mouse (Old World), left, and a deer mouse (New World)

Drawing of the cleverly fashioned nest of a harvest mouse

having gray or brown fur, a long scaly or hairy tail, and large ears.

New World mice are residents of fields and forests. As a result, few men and women have seen a delicate deer mouse peer out from behind a log, raise its big ears in response to a strange sound, and then scurry to safety. Nor have many city dwellers experienced the thrill of finding the cleverly fashioned nest of a tiny harvest mouse on the top of a grass stem. Actually, because many species of New World mice prefer to set up housekeeping in secluded places, only trained naturalists can spot them as they engage in various activities. On the other hand, one Old World mouse is familiar to people in all parts of the world. This well-known but far from popular creature is the house mouse.

Generally speaking, the fur coats of Old World mice are more attractive than those of the New World kin. This is because the fur of Old World mice varies greatly in texture and color.

Common in northern Africa where it is often kept as a pet, the Barbary mouse is most attractive. Its grayish-fawn fur is barred with ten longitudinal brown stripes that run along the sides and back.

Some species have silky or woolly fur. The fur of others is spiny or prickly. Still others have skins "not much more substantial than wet toilet paper," sparsely covered with little wiry hairs. In contrast to the many species that are dull brown, gray, or gray-brown, a species native to West Africa is covered with white spots, while the Barbary mouse wears a brightly striped coat. There are also albino, black-and-white, black-and-gray, and pie-bald mice.

The ways and wiles of mice vary even more than the coloration of Old World species. Mice, one of the most versatile of animals, have adapted to life underground, in trees, on sand dunes, in salt marshes, and between the walls of buildings. Even before mice unknowingly began to be transported to distant lands by man, certain mice native to Asia had reached Australia—the only land mammals except the bat to accomplish this feat. Zoologists believe the mice made the journey from Asia to the Island Continent on logs that offered little shelter from the buffeting of waves and wind. No wonder both Old and New World mice prosper almost everywhere, despite worldwide efforts to exterminate them!

2. Mouse Lore

" 'Tis an old tale, and often told."—Scott

According to ancient belief, the first mice fell to Earth from the heavens during a violent storm. Some early Germans claimed that witches fashioned mice out of cloth, while others thought they concocted them from potent herbs brewed in huge kettles. As this secret potion seethed and bubbled, the witches chanted, *"Maus, Maus, heraus in Taufels Namen!* (Mouse, mouse, come out in the Devil's name)," whereupon mice would leap out of the kettle.

European legend maintains that Satan created the first mice while plotting to sink Noah's Ark. The Prince of Darkness is also said to have assumed the form of a mouse, and, were it not for Noah's cats, would have gnawed a hole in the Ark's hull. Although this plot failed—so the story goes—the Devil has delighted in disguising himself as a mouse ever since.

Not only Europeans associate the mouse with evil. In the Near East, the people employ it as a symbol of vileness and rapacity. In fact, the mouse is held to be a creature of ill omen throughout the world.

In the ancient city of Troy, an image of a mouse was kept in Apollo's temple. He was held to be both the protector and destroyer of mice.

Despite its evil reputation, the mouse has played an important part in religion. It was closely allied with Apollo, a major Greek god who was believed to have a special interest in agriculture. Actually, Apollo's relationship with mice was contradictory. Although he was said to destroy those that infested farms, he was at the same time held to be the rodents' protector. This is why an image of a mouse stood in Apollo's temple in the city of Troy and cages containing white mice were kept under the altar.

Evidently Apollo did not exterminate mice as fast as certain of his worshipers wished. So some of them followed the advice given in an ancient book on farming.

> Take a sheet of paper and write on it as follows: "I adjure, ye mice here present, that you neither injure me nor suffer another mouse to do so. I give you yonder field (here specify the field) but if I ever catch you here again, by the mother of the gods I will rend you in several pieces." Write this, and stick the paper on an unhewned stone in the field before sunrise, taking care to keep the written side up.

The Old Testament calls mice unclean and forbids the Jews to eat their flesh. However, early Jews—along with other ancient

17

One of the most attractive mutant color varieties of mice used in genetic research is the golden-brown strain known to scientists as DBA. These initials stand for "dilute brown agouti." However, except for the brilliant hue of their coats, these mice have nothing in common with the practically tailless agoutis that inhabit forests from southern Mexico to Brazil.

peoples—venerated mice. The Jews also expressed their gratitude to the mice God sent to plague the Phillistines who had stolen the sacred Torah from the Israelites' camp. The story of the theft of the holy scroll and of its return with a reparation of five golden mice is recounted in the Book of Samuel in the Bible.

While the natives of the island of Bali do not actually worship mice, they endow them with special powers and take care not to offend them. Although Balinese farmers kill vast numbers of mice when hordes of the rodents ravage their fields, they always capture two mice alive. These are treated with great respect, given a gift, and then ceremoniously released. As the mice dash to freedom, the onlookers bow down to them as if they were divinities.

Perhaps the most widespread superstition concerning mice is the belief that the soul leaves the body in the form of a mouse during sleep. The credulous believe that if the sleeper awakes before the mouse (soul) returns, he will die. Thus it is widely held that it is extremely dangerous to awaken a person—his soul may be scampering about somewhere in the guise of a mouse.

In Transylvania, the Romanian province famous as the home of Dracula, children are not allowed to sleep with their mouths

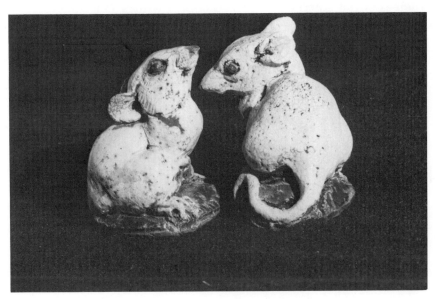

Two ceramic mice by Anne Philbrick Hall

Many people believe that the soul emerges from the body at death in the form of a mouse. If the mouse is black, the deceased is considered to have been a sinner. Picture by Lear.

open. The parents fear that their souls will wiggle out between their teeth as mice and the youngsters will never wake.

Many peoples are convinced that the soul emerges from the body in the guise of a mouse at death as well as during sleep. In times past, it was thought that if the soul turned into a red mouse, the deceased had led a virtuous life. If the soul was transformed into a black mouse, it was considered a sign that a sinner had died.

Mice universally have been associated with death. The belief that mice flee a house just before one of its occupants dies is common to peoples everywhere. So is the contention that if a mouse nibbles the clothes of a sleeping person, that individual will soon die. Not only do Europeans regard mice as forerunners of death but also as carriers of misfortune—the more mice seen, the greater the impending calamity. For example, the French claim it is a sure sign of the outbreak of a war when great numbers of mice appear.

20

On the other hand, the inhabitants of Bohemia in western Czechoslovakia delight in seeing mice—providing they are white. When Bohemians see a white mouse, they supply it with food so that it will not leave and take good luck with it.

Ever since classical times, the mouse has been accused of having the evil eye and thus being capable of bringing harm to any animal or person it looks at intently. The list of amulets designed to counteract the baleful spells supposedly cast by mice is a long one. One of the most unusual was a coin minted by the Greeks that depicted a mouse. The Greeks reasoned that the coin would flatter mice and thus keep them from casting evil spells.

Today, superstitious Greeks are positive a famine will soon occur if mice gnaw holes in bags of flour. Meanwhile, Jewish tradition states that eating any food touched by a mouse will cause either forgetfulness or a sore throat.

However, early doctors believed that mice had medicinal value. They compounded them into prescriptions designed to cure a long list of ills. Pliny, the great Roman naturalist, recommended a plaster of mouse ashes and honey to relieve headache

Bohemians believe that white mice are lucky.

and claimed that the same mixture made an excellent mouth-wash. Pliny also maintained that the mouth would be "made agreeable" if the teeth were rubbed with the ashes of a mouse mixed with honey.

Long before Pliny wrote his famous *Historia Naturalis*, Egyptians physicians were giving medicines containing the ashes, blood, fat, flesh, or skins of mice to their patients. Evidently the doctors in the Valley of the Nile were convinced that pre-scriptions which included parts of mice were particularly effica-cious for children's diseases—examinations of the stomachs of many Egyptian children mummified thousands of years ago re-veal the remains of mice.

Until comparatively recent time, mouse pie was served both in the Old World and in parts of the Americas to children who suffered from small pox, whooping cough, and measles in hopes of effecting a cure. Fried mice were also fed to youngsters with kidney ailments.

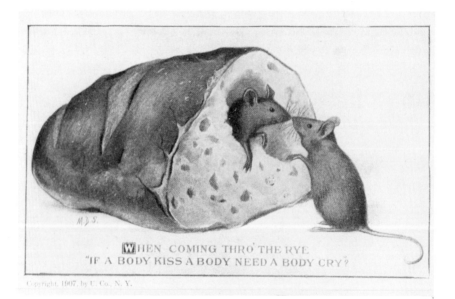

WHEN COMING THRO' THE RYE
"IF A BODY KISS A BODY NEED A BODY CRY?

In spite of universal bad feelings about mice, they were often featured on comic postcards in the early twentieth century.

At one time it was the practice to rub mouse fat over the body to ward off paralysis. During this period, doctors were convinced that the best method of removing a wart was to plaster it with the fat of a swan sprinkled with mouse dung ashes. Mouse dung itself was thought to have outstanding medicinal properties. Diluted with water, it was used to reduce swellings; mixed with honey, it was employed to "unite bones"; rubbed on the body, it was said to prevent internal disorders.

Both ancient and medieval doctors were convinced that infected wounds and lung complaints could be best treated if a mouse—preferably a specimen from Africa—was skinned, boiled in its own oil, salted, and eaten. However, physicians and patients alike were positive that anyone who carried the tips of a mouse's ears in a red cloth would rarely need any medicine. It was understood, however, that this amulet would not protect the wearer from illness unless the tips of the ears had been cropped from a live mouse. Moreover, the mouse had to be set free after the operation.

Centuries ago, toothaches were relieved by stuffing ashes of mouse dung into cavities. While this custom has vanished, peoples throughout the world believe that mice have tremendous influence on the development of human teeth. When children in central Europe "lose" a first tooth, their parents immediately drop the tooth down a mouse hole to prevent toothache. Another common practice is to put "milk teeth" where they are apt to be seen by mice. For example, natives of South Pacific islands throw their children's milk teeth into the thatch that roofs their huts. Parents who put children's teeth where they think mice will find them hope that the rodents will carry them away. If they do, the parents are convinced their offspring's new teeth will be as strong as those of mice.

Mice scamper across the pages of world literature. Perhaps the earliest written stories detailing the adventures of mice are found in the *Panchatantra*, a collection of fables compiled about A.D. 500. Like the majority of the tales early Greek and Roman authors wrote about mice, the fables in the *Panchatantra* are known only to a few. On the other hand, the fables attributed to Aesop (620–564 B.C.) are as popular today as they were in ancient times.

Aesop employs the mouse to teach a moral lesson in several

Many painters have illustrated Aesop's fable about the lion and the mouse. This fanciful picture originally was drawn by Jean Ignace Isidore Gerard, French early-nineteenth-century caricaturist known by the pseudonym of Grandville.

of his fables. None of these is better known than "The Lion and the Mouse," in which a lion, rudely awakened by a mouse, graciously releases it without harm. Sometime later the lion is caught in a net spread by hunters and roars in anger. Recognizing the roar, the mouse hurries to the spot, cuts the net with its sharp teeth, and sets the lion free. The lesson Aesop teaches in this story is that no act of kindness, no matter how small, ever goes unrewarded.

Interestingly enough, tribal storytellers among the Indians who roamed the Great Plains made the same use of a mouse that Aesop did. In their accounts, a mouse that was aided by a legendary hero repays its benefactor by helping him overcome an evil giant elk.

Long before children are old enough to read Aesop's mouse fables, many are learning nursery rhymes. Two of the most popular deal with mice. One details what happened when a mouse ran up a clock. The other tells of the three blind mice whose tails were cut off by the farmer's wife. Originally, both these rhymes were employed to teach children to count. It was not until 1744 that they appeared in a book.

Young adults who delight in horror stories should revel in a medieval tale in which mice play important roles. This thriller recounts how a heartless miser bought up all the grain during a famine, stored it in a tower, and was selling the grain at a tremendous profit when a horde of starving mice swept into the tower, ate the grain, and devoured the miser.

Tradition places the miser's tower on an island in the Rhine River near Bingen, Germany. However, it is doubtful that this tower—which was built as a toll station—ever held grain. The chances are the legend of a miser being eaten by mice stems from confusing the German *maut* (toll) with *maus* (mouse).

Mice are mentioned in the Bible, praised and insulted in Shakespeare's plays, and are the central figures in short stories by many authors, including Chekhov, Eugene Field, Kafka, H. H. Munro ("Saki"), and William Saroyan. While the list of authors who have written about mice is lengthy, a catalog of the poets who have been inspired by mice is far longer. It includes Byron, Lindsay, Millay, Pope, Southey, and Whitman.

Undoubtedly the best-known bit from any poem dealing with the mouse is Robert Burns's "The best-laid schemes o' mice an' men gang aft agley," which is quoted when matters do not work

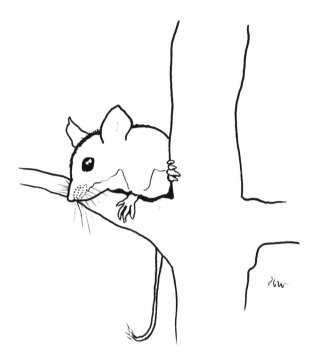

Mice appear in many proverbs and literary works. Drawing by Peter Weber.

out as expected. Burns is also responsible for describing the mouse as a "Wee, sleekit, cow'rin', tim'rous beastie."

While the mouse in Clement Moore's "A Visit from St. Nicholas" does not stir, a mouse in another Christmas poem is very active. It is also very clever. Emilie Poulson makes this clear in "Santa Claus and the Mouse." When Santa claims he has filled a stocking to overflowing and challenges a mouse to "put in one thing more," the mouse gnaws a tiny hole in the stocking!

Mice are featured in numerous proverbs. "When the cat's away the mice will play" is probably the best known. This proverb—employed to describe misbehavior in the absence of authority—occurs in one form or another in every European language. Several other proverbs that mention mice are also universally used.

27

All over the world children are warned to be "Quiet as a mouse," while anyone without funds is said to be "Poor as a church mouse."

Not only are church mice proverbially penniless but also they are supposedly starving, as "Hungry as a church mouse" indicates. The origin of this proverb goes back to the days when no food was stored or served in churches. Meanwhile, although there is considerable truth to "No house without mouse" and "No larder but has its mice," both these adages can be used to imply that flaws can be found in anything.

The English are particularly fond of mouse proverbs. They ridicule an unworkable idea with "Can a mouse fall in love with a cat?" and advise the overly modest "Don't make yourself a mouse or the cat will eat you." When someone insists on continuing to argue after making his point, the English say, "Pour not water on a drowning mouse." Individuals who are sophisticated but pretend innocence are bluntly told, "You have daily to do with the Devil, and pretend to be frightened of a mouse."

In Denmark the foolhearty are checked with " 'Tis a bold mouse that makes its nest in a cat's ear." The Spanish "The mice do not play with the cat's son" is used to express fears that someone is going to benefit at the expense of others. In several countries, variations of the French "A mouse must not seek to cast a shadow like an elephant" is applied to those attempting too much. When the Chinese feel that an individual is too ambitious, they say, "A mouse can drink no more than its fill from a river."

The need to be prepared for every contingency is summed up by the Latin *"Mus non uni fidit antro."* There are at least a dozen versions of this proverb, which can be freely translated, "A mouse never trusts its life to one hole." Another ancient proverb that has many forms is the Greek "The mouse is in the brine." It is used when a person falls into difficulties through his own deeds.

Ever since Mickey Mouse scampered off Walt Disney's drawing board some fifty years ago, his adventures have delighted children and adults alike.

Famous artists have neglected the mouse. The only master of the brush to place a mouse prominently on canvas was Fiegel of Germany. However, mice have been a favorite model of cartoonists and illustrators of children's books. The most famous mice to jump off a drawing board are, of course, Walt Disney's Mickey and Minnie.

Collecting figurines depicting mice has become a popular hobby. Most of these figurines are machine made and therefore inexpensive. But skilled artisans have also carved mice out of ivory, fashioned them from glass and precious metals, and molded them in stone and bronze. Perhaps the most celebrated sculpture of a mouse was the statue raised to commemorate the victory of Sethes of Egypt over the Assyrians. Because legend holds that, the night before the battle, mice ate the bow strings, quivers, and shield thongs of the Assyrians, forcing them to retreat in panic, Sethes was depicted holding a mouse in his hand.

29

This porcelain sculpture by Kazmar depicts a young badger stalking a field mouse. Although the badger—the name is derived from the "badges" or markings on the face and head—is a young cub, the mouse is in great danger.

Generally speaking, composers have shown no more interest in mice than artists. However, the three blind mice, the frog that went a'courting, the mouse under the queen's chair, and a few other fictional mice have inspired music-makers. Among these make-believe creatures is the seven-headed mouse king, the villain in *The Nutcracker*, the most fanciful of ballets, whose music was written by Tschaikovsky. Because *The Nutcracker* enthralls children, it is usually performed during the Christmas season when school is not in session.

Common speech makes good use of the word mouse. Actors call inferior plays and poorly constructed theaters "mousetraps," while oil drillers apply the same term to the tool with which

30

they cut or retrieve ropes caught in an oil well. In addition to employing such phrases as "quiet as a mouse," many individuals refer to a black eye as a "mouse."

To a miner, "mouse eaten" refers to quartz that is full of holes. Professional burglars call a petty thief a "mouser." When a person stops and carefully considers whether or not he should take a certain action, his companions may poke fun at his hesitation and ask, "Are you a man or a mouse?" This jeering taunt often provokes anger, but no young lady should be upset if she is called "mouse"—a term of endearment that has been used for over two hundred years.

One of the most exciting moments in The Nutcracker *is the dance of the wicked Mouse King as he leads his troops into battle.*

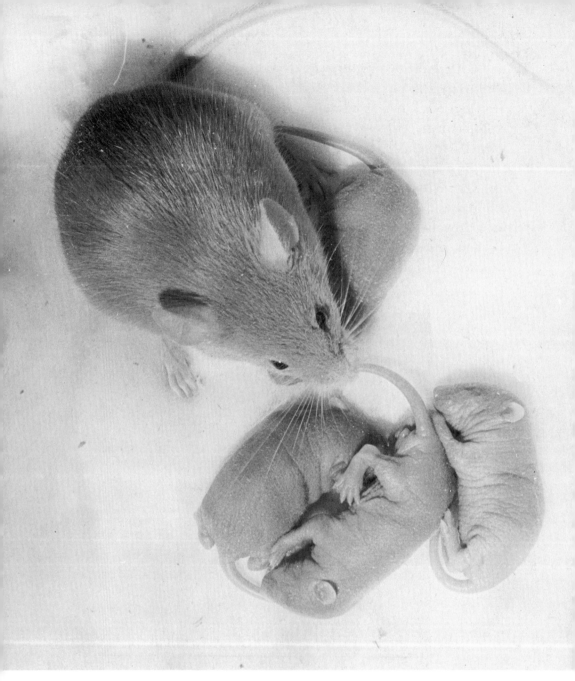

Naked, blind, and helpless, these newborn house-mouse pups will develop rapidly and, within a few weeks, raise families of their own.

3. House Mice

"I had as lief have their room as their company."—Green

Man has been matching wits with the house mouse for centuries. *Mus musculus* has learned that it is far easier to find food and shelter in human habitations than to live in the open. Probably the most widely distributed rodent, the house mouse is an unwelcome boarder in buildings throughout the world. Not only does it eat and spoil food needed by humans but also it taints a long list of manufactured articles.

Zoologists once thought that the house mouse—along with the common rat—evolved in central Asia. However, research tends to confirm that the house mouse's original range included the Mediterranean area, southern Europe, North Africa, and the steppes of Asia as far east as Japan. Today, as indicated, the house mouse is found wherever humans live. It thrives in all climates with the exception of the frigid polar regions.

The growth of international commerce enabled *musculus* to extend its original range. Traders carried the house mouse aboard their vessels as a stowaway and unloaded it with their cargo. The house mouse was unknown in the New World until about the time of the American Revolution, when it arrived on ships from Europe. House mice have also been transported overland from one country to another in wheeled vehicles and trains. Today, the airplane provides them with a swift and comfortable passage to new homes.

Mus musculus is well named—*musculus* means "little mouse" in Latin. House mice certainly are tiny, weighing about an ounce. The head and body length is between three and four inches. The scale-ringed, practically hairless tail is approximately the same length. House mice have pointed muzzles equipped with sensitive whiskers that enable them to determine the width of an opening before they venture into it. They have moderately large ears and bright beady eyes. The soft fur of most specimens is brownish-gray above—a coloration commonly called "mouse gray"—with slightly paler fur on the underparts. However, the interbreeding of various subspecies of house mice has resulted in some individuals that wear dark, light, or spotted fur coats of various colors.

Despite their big bright eyes, mice do not have keen sight. Actually, they are nearsighted. Some authorities believe that house mice cannot distinguish an object more than two inches

House mice by Peter Weber

away in daylight. Current studies indicate that house mice do have a degree of night vision, which may explain why they are mainly nocturnal.

As house mice move quickly and silently through a building and climb rapidly up walls fashioned of brick and cement, they rely on their senses of smell and hearing to warn them of danger. When threatened, a house mouse runs for the safety of its nearest hole, wiggling through openings less than half an inch in diameter. If no hole is handy and its escape route is blocked, *musculus* may make a spectacular leap over the barrier.

Usually the sharp ears of a house mouse give it ample warning of approaching danger. Not only do house mice have the ability to detect faint noises but also they employ ultrasonics when communicating with one another. While humans can hear some of their squeaks, most sounds made by house mice are too high pitched for our ears to catch.

While investigating this use of ultrasonics, scientists discovered that when a finger was rubbed along the top of its glass cage, a house mouse's ears would move in time with the finger. If the rubbing was continued for a considerable period, the mouse became very excited. Some individuals dashed about as if dancing, suffered a seizure, and died.

Incidentally, the "Japanese waltzing mice" sold in pet stores really do not waltz or perform any type of dance. They do run in circles constantly. This is because a malformity of their ears affects their sense of balance.

House mice usually live in buildings where they are protected from cold and from all of their foes except man and rats. With the coming of spring, house mice frequently move into "summer homes." During the hot months they may sublet the burrows of other small animals, nest beneath thick vegetation, or live below a fallen tree. With the approach of chilly weather, the mice return to their original residences.

While the house mice are living outdoors they are preyed upon by a long list of enemies including birds, foxes, rats, snakes, weasels, and the domestic cat. A house mouse cannot successfully defend itself against any of these predators. Its most aggressive act is to face a foe, stand on the hindlegs while holding the forelegs together as if praying, and point the nose upward. Few mouse hunters are scared off by this pose. Nor can house mice compete with the field mice they encounter during their summer "vacations." When the two meet, field mice either drive their city cousins away or kill them. No wonder the life span of a house mouse is about three years!

Whether they are spending the winter in a warm building or camping outdoors in the summer, house mice establish territories and mark their limits with urine. This habit explains the "mousy smell" often detected in boarded-up or abandoned houses. This odor is also evident in laboratories where captive mice are kept. Whenever the cages are made sterile and fresh smelling, their occupants immediately mark them again.

Mice living in a specific territory recognize each other through their sense of smell—each group having a characteristic odor. Thus if a mouse accidentally wanders into a strange territory it is detected immediately and driven away. However, laboratory

Note that although this baby mouse has not yet grown any hair, its whiskers are fully developed.

experiments have shown that if the newcomer is artificially scented with the accepted odor, it is welcomed.

When food is abundant, predators few, and man's traps and poisons ineffectual, the population of a mouse colony rapidly increases and, within a short time, the territory is overpopulated. When this occurs the males of the colony battle for supremacy. Eventually, one male becomes dominant and he alone mates with the females. Because the dominant male is unable to sire as many litters as all the males combined, the number of births in the colony is reduced and further overcrowding prevented.

House mice breed through most of the year. Indeed, the survival of the house mouse is due as much to its breeding rate as to its skill in finding food and shelter.

After mating, a female selects a protected spot and fashions a nest from scraps of cloth or other soft fibrous materials. While house mice living in warehouses where food is stored may have as many as ten litters a year, the average female has only five. Usually, each litter is composed of five young.

Called "pups" by scientists, baby mice are born naked and blind approximately three weeks after their parents mate. The youngsters are weaned in eighteen days. When they are six weeks old, they begin to raise families of their own.

Although fundamentally seed and grain eaters, house mice consume a wide variety of foods ranging from flour to meat. As indicated, this is one of the reasons why they prosper in so many different environments. However, house mice that have been accustomed to "panhandling" humans may find it impossible to survive on natural foods if their customary sources of supply disappear. When the thirty-six human residents of St. Kilda abandoned their island homes and moved to the Scottish mainland in 1930, the house mice that had depended upon these inhabitants to furnish them with food became extinct.

Meanwhile, in nearly every part of the world, house mice

All mice and rats are gnawing animals.

consume huge stores of valuable food stuffs. But the amount of grain, meat, and produce eaten by these rodents is minute compared to the vast quantity of food they render unsuitable for human consumption by contamination.

Technically, members of the genus Microtus *are voles but they are commonly called meadow mice. The great numbers of species of field mice closely resemble one another but occupy a wide range of habitats.* Microtus ochrogaster *shown here is known as the prairie meadow mouse.*

*Typical of the group of small rodents popularly called field mice, the meadow mouse (*Microtus pennsylvanicus*) is widespread. It is the most common and prolific of our native rodents as well as one of the most destructive.*

4. Field Mice

"There's no love lost between us."—Goldsmith

There are approximately three hundred species of field mice. All have the same general appearance, although their popular names differ. The rodents commonly called field mice in the United States are termed voles in England, while those larger species that live near water are known as water rats in northern Europe.

Circumpolar in distribution, field mice are found from the Arctic barrens to southern Europe and the Himalaya Mountains in Asia, and to Central America in the New World. With the exception of extremely arid areas, field mice abound in most parts of the United States.

Bogs, damp woodlands, gardens, grassy patches on the tundra, marshes, meadows, suburban back yards, stream banks, swamps, and stands of stunted vegetation above the timberline are among the favorite habitats of field mice. Certain species prefer high ground. Others are semiaquatic, diving and swimming with great skill.

The meadow mouse *(Microtus pennsylvanicus)* is typical of

41

the rodents commonly known as field mice. *Pennsylvanicus* is rather large, ranging from six to eight inches in length including the short tail, and weighing about four ounces. Heavily proportioned, with stocky legs, the meadow mouse stands approximately two inches high at the shoulder. The head is rounded, eyes small and beady. Water-repellent, coarse, dark-brown or gray fur (which almost covers the small, rounded ears) becomes lighter on the underparts.

Pennsylvanicus has three claims to fame. Not only is it the most common and prolific of North American rodents but also it is one of the most destructive. In order to satisfy its ravenous appetite, a meadow mouse, like all field mice, must eat its own weight in food daily. As a result, these mice are active day and night—taking only short naps—seeking "almost anything that grows." Although vegetation makes up most of its diet, the meadow mouse does eat some insects.

Meadow mice hoard in underground vaults any food they are unable to eat. To insure that their stomachs will be full during the winter, the mice store large amounts of food in these chambers during the cool days of autumn. While eating or gathering food, meadow mice, again like all field mice, destroy bulbs planted by gardeners, chew the bark off fruit trees, ruin vegetable plantings, dine on reaped grain, nibble root crops, and compete with cattle for alfalfa, clover, and other green plant food.

During their constant quest for food, meadow mice lay out an intricate system of paths about an inch wide. These trails extend from their nests and underground chambers through their feeding areas. Some are above ground, others are below the surface. Still others are tunneled beneath snow. The winter is the only season when meadow mice can seek food without fear of being seen by predators. This is because in winter they either feed on stored food or forage under the snow.

Although each mouse lays out its own pathways, these roads

Normally an acre of land is inhabited by ten to thirty meadow mice. But when food is plentiful, the meadow-mouse population rises dramatically and an acre may contain as many as 12,000 meadow mice. This specimen was photographed in Alaska.

are used by all its neighbors. Therefore, keeping these smoothly worn runways clear of twigs and pebbles is a joint effort—the mice want no obstruction in their way if they have to dash for safety.

Because the meadow mouse is constantly active, it consumes

Owls make very little noise when flying and have such keen hearing that they can find their prey in total darkness. As a result, these winged predators destroy untold millions of mice annually. "Screech Owl and Mouse" by Dr. William Turner. Note tail of mouse disappearing into the stump.

a tremendous amount of energy. As a result, the average female rarely lives more than a year, while the lifespan of a few males may be about eighteen months. The reason females do not live as long as males is that they not only wear themselves out looking for food but they also are weakened from the care and feeding of so many babies.

Meadow mice are very prolific. There are usually young in the nest from January to December. The nest itself may be a globelike structure hidden in a tussock of grass or sheltered by a log. Because these mice dislike warm weather, they often move into underground quarters when the temperature rises above 85°F. (30°C.). Usually, the nests in underground chambers are constructed from dry grass.

Female meadow mice mate for the first time when a month old and have a litter every twenty-one days thereafter. A single female may produce as many as seventeen litters of four to nine babies in a year. Born helpless, blind, and naked, the pups are fully furred within four days and, when two weeks old, leave the nest.

No creature is more preyed upon than meadow mice. At night owls feast upon them, while other birds of prey and gulls dine on them during the day. So does a long list of animals ranging from skunks to grizzly bears. Snapping turtles and some fish also consider them a treat. Were it not for its high rate of reproduction, the meadow mouse probably would become extinct.

Despite predators, parasites, and disease, the number of meadow mice in a specific area may increase incredibly. Zoologists estimate that, under normal conditions, thirty meadow mice inhabit an acre of land. But, in what Europeans call a "vole year," the population may rise to twelve thousand meadow mice per acre. When this occurs, all vegetation is destroyed.

Fortunately, when the meadow mouse population peaks, natural enemies also increase in numbers. This, plus the inroads of disease and the lack of sufficient food for all, soon reduces the meadow mouse population below its normal size. However, within four years, there will be another "mouse plague."

A *resident of eastern forests, the American pine vole* (Pitymys pinetorum) *does extensive damage to the roots of fruit trees.*

Adult female northern grasshopper mouse. Leucogaster *is a bold hunter and preys on a long list of insects that damage crops.*

5. Hunters and Harvesters

"He that would eat the fruit must climb the tree."—Scotch Proverb

Mice go to great lengths to obtain food. The pine mouse *(Pitymys pinetorum)*, when looking for edible roots, often takes short cuts through tunnels dug by moles. The beach mouse *(Peromyscus polionotus niveiventris)*, a resident of the Florida coast, will nest under palm fronds on a sand dune in order to be near the sea oats on which it feeds.

Many mice are harvesters, reaping both wild plants and cultivated crops. These rodents have adaptions that enable them to strip vegetation and to carry supplies to their storehouses. Still other mice scorn a vegetarian diet. Meat eaters, they hunt for their food.

Grasshopper Mice

No man-eating tigers are more ferocious than the southern grasshopper mouse *(Onychomys torridus)* and the northern grasshopper mouse *(Onychomys leucogaster)*. Bold hunters, these mice not only prey on grasshoppers but also on ants, beetles, butterflies, crickets, cutworms, moths, and spiders. They also stalk "big game" and easily kill mice of several species and vanquish scorpions. Because the southern grasshopper mouse is so skilled in killing scorpions, it has been nicknamed the "scorpion mouse."

While grasshopper mice are the only North American rodents that feed primarily on flesh, they do consume a very small amount of vegetation. But they do little harm to man and must be credited with being outstanding natural regulators of insect-pest populations.

The northern grasshopper mouse's range extends from northwestern North America south to Mexico. *Torridus*—the southern grasshopper mouse—lives in the dry Southwest. Both species often inhabit the same general area but have no contact. This is because *torridus* nests on low-lying ground while its relative nests on high ground.

Grasshopper mice are quite attractive. Their fur resembles velvet and is delicately colored. That of the northern species is buff on the back and top of the head while the rest of the pelage is snow white. *Torridus* is also bicolored. Its head, back and upper sides are pale brown to grayish or pinkish cinnamon, and the underparts are white.

Both of these stocky mice—the northern grasshopper mouse is the larger—have relatively short, thick tails whose tips are usually white. Interestingly enough, the tail of *leucogaster* is normally less than half the body length, while the tail of the southern grasshopper mouse is usually more than half the body length.

Grasshopper mice are nocturnal hunters. But they may prefer to go hungry rather than to hunt if the moon is bright or a heavy rain is falling. Overcast damp nights are their favorite "hunting season." Not only does the dampness make it easier for them to pick up the spoor of potential prey but also poor visibility gives the mice some protection from night-roving predators.

When grasshopper mice leave their burrows at dusk, they sniff the ground like hound dogs chasing a fox. Once a fresh scent is detected, the mice follow it, "barking" in a series of short, sharp squeaks or uttering a shrill whistle. Once within striking distance, these deadly killers leap onto their victims and sink their long, sharp teeth into the throat or the head. Small mammals are slaughtered by being bitten at the base of the skull until the spinal cord is severed.

Southern grasshopper mice butcher scorpions by repeatedly biting the tail until it is immobilized and then attacking the head. *Torridus* is equally adept at overpowering those beetles that shoot a poison spray at their enemies from the tip of the abdomen. To avoid this secretion, *torridus* holds the beetle in its forepaws and jams the abdomen into the ground. Incidentally, the southern grasshopper mouse is able to survive in arid areas because of the high water content of the animal flesh on which it feeds.

Despite the dependence of grasshopper mice on meat, they eat seeds and also store them for future use. Because the grasshopper-mouse population in a given locale is usually quite low, these mice rarely have to compete for food. However, there is a bitter rivalry between individuals. Males are ever ready to defend their territories, which they claim by standing on their hind legs, raising their heads high, and uttering a high-pitched call. To impregnate the ground with their scent, grasshopper mice also sink shallow shafts, in which they roll, throughout their territories. The northern grasshopper mouse also takes these dust baths to keep its fur clean and in a non-oily condition.

Boxing matches in which the opponents stand on their hind legs and pummel each other are common. So are fierce battles between dominant males and their subordinates. Females may fight with their mates and bite them to death.

Although grasshopper mice can excavate burrows quickly, they often sublet the deserted homes of gophers, ground squirrels, and other animals. If the mice do dig their own burrows, they are apt to make spacious "apartments." One section is used as a dining room and nursery, another as a retreat to which the mice flee in time of danger. A third section serves as a pantry where the mice store seed. Whether their homes are large or small, grasshopper mice always excavate a chamber which they use as a toilet.

As indicated, grasshopper mice are extremely vocal. Their repertoire not only consists of hunting calls and territorial advertisements but also of a wide range of chirps and squeaks em-

Like its northern relative, the southern grasshopper mouse feeds primarily on flesh. Because of its skill in killing scorpions, torridus *has been nicknamed the "scorpion mouse."*

ployed during courtship, grooming, and fighting, and to express alarm.

Most of our knowledge of the reproduction of grasshopper mice has been gained from laboratory investigation. Research scientists have learned that most captive female grasshopper mice produce their first litters during the breeding season following the year of birth. There are three to six litters a year, each consisting of four or five babies which weigh one-tenth of an ounce at birth. When ten days old, their eyes are open and they are capable of eating seeds and bits of insects. The pups now pass the time grooming themselves and fighting. When about a month old, they are capable of fending for themselves.

Experimentation has revealed that the reproduction of the southern grasshopper mouse closely parallels that of its northern cousin. Perhaps the most fascinating fact that has emerged from the controlled breeding of *torridus* is that the male is a devoted parent. However, the female drives her mate from the nest immediately after she gives birth and does not allow him to return for about three days. When readmitted, the proud father grooms the pups, huddles over them protectively, and helps the female retrieve any youngsters that wander too far away. If an intruder threatens their family, both parents shriek a war cry and launch an attack.

Harvest Mice

There are many species of harvest mice. While only one of these is found in Europe, nearly seventy species and subspecies inhabit the Americas. The most common New World harvest mice are the Eastern harvest mouse *(Reithrodontomys humulis)* and the Western harvest mouse *(Reithrodontomys megalotis)*. These seed eaters have a wide distribution, being found from the eastern United States to the Pacific coast and from the Dakotas southward to northern South America.

Inhabiting arid areas, the Western harvest mouse, like its eastern kin, builds a ball-like nest attached to grass stalks.

Harvest mice are delicate and graceful creatures. Their scientific names are almost as long as their bodies. The European species is only two inches in length and weighs about a third of an ounce. New World harvest mice—which weigh three ounces—are slightly larger than their Old World counterparts but are smaller than the common house mouse, which they resemble at first glance. Harvest mice can be distinguished from house mice by their tails, which are quite hairy.

The fur coats of harvest mice are grayish or brown and shade into a lighter buff or gray on the sides, with white or pinkish-white underparts. The round ears are relatively large, the medium-sized eyes a sparkling black. Because their feet are adapted for climbing, harvest mice can run up stalks with ease. As the stalks bend under their weight, the mice swing their tails from side to side "very much like a tight-rope walker with his long pole." The tail not only helps the mice to keep their balance but also can be curled around a stalk to serve as a support.

No circus acrobats are more agile than harvest mice. These tiny rodents show tremendous skill as they scamper up stalks

The harvest mouse curls its long tail around a stem for support.

swaying in brisk winds in order to reach the seed heads. When feeding, they hold fast to the stem with the hind legs, grip it with the tail, and use the forepaws as "rakes" to gather the seeds. After harvesting all the seeds, they swing like trapeze artists to a nearby stalk and reap its crop.

Harvest mice are outstanding architects. Most species weave globular nests several inches in diameter from coarse grasses. These may be slung between two or three stalks a few inches above the ground or fastened to a bush high in the air. When completed, a harvest mouse's nest is a perfect sphere capable of withstanding driving rains and strong winds. A little round hole—usually on the underside—serves as an entrance to the interior which is lined with finely shredded plant material.

Certain harvest mice dig burrows in which they hide their nests. Others take up residence in excavations made by woodpeckers in trees or in holes in fence posts. Still others remodel deserted birds' nests. But no matter where their nests are located, harvest mice remain in them until twilight. As the daylight fades, they set out to find food, always returning home before sunrise.

Normally, harvest mice breed twice a year, the mating season running from April to September. During this period the males "sing" a love song to the females—a shrill cry that is almost inaudible to the human ear. Approximately three weeks after mating, three to seven babies are born. Although they weigh one-twentieth of an ounce or less at birth, they are fully grown when five weeks old.

Although harvest mice begin raising families when only three months old, they have always been relatively rare. This is the reason why the European harvest mouse was not noticed by

This harvest mouse nest was lithographed by Louis Prang in Boston a century ago.

The eastern harvest mouse has a shorter tail than the western harvest mouse, center, or the fulvous harvest mouse, which has the longest of the three. By Jane O'Regan after Grossenheider.

any naturalist until the late eighteenth century. Today, the harvest mouse population on both sides of the Atlantic is declining. Not only have modern farming methods destroyed much of the harvest mouse's habitat but also their food supply has been reduced—machinery reaps standing crops far more efficiently than did the hand-held scythes of yesteryear.

Pocket Mice

Although pocket mice are among the smallest of mammals—the Pacific pocket mouse is the tiniest of rodents—they are extremely efficient harvesters. Because of differences in body structure, the fifty-odd species of these minute vegetarians have been divided into two groups. The larger of these contains the silky pocket mice—residents of dry areas from southwest Canada to central America—that comprise the genus *Perognathus*. Scientists have split the second group into two categories—the genera *Liomys* and *Heteromys*. The former includes the spiny pocket mice, inhabitants of arid regions from Texas to Central America. Forest pocket mice, which live in forests from Mexico to Panama, make up the other category.

Pocket mice get their common name from their fur-lined cheek pouches. These external pockets of skin open on either side of the small mouth. Each pouch holds from one-eighth to one-half a teaspoon of grass, leaves, seeds, or nesting material, depending upon the species.

Generally speaking, all pocket mice have large, broad heads, small, rounded ears, and rather long tails which often end in hairy tufts. Certain pocket mice have tails as long or longer than the combined length of head and body (two to five inches). Spiny pocket mice are slightly larger than silky pocket mice, while forest pocket mice are the largest of the three. The length of the head and body is between five and six inches while the tail may be eight inches long.

As their name implies, silky pocket mice have soft, shining fur. On the other hand, the fur of spiny pocket mice is rather coarse and has stiff, flattened bristles scattered through it. The fur varies greatly in color. Some pocket mice are pale yellow

Approximately fifty species of terrestrial and nocturnal mice are protected by sharp spines which evolved from soft hairs. The Cairo spiny mouse shown here—first identified near Cairo, Egypt, in the early nineteenth century—has a wide range that extends from India through southwest Asia, to much of Africa.

or gray above and white underneath. Others wear coats of different shades of buff. Still others may be whitish or black.

If a pocket mouse's coloration blends with its surroundings, the chances of attack by predators is greatly reduced. This is why certain pocket mice in New Mexico stay within a limited area. The pocket mice that live within the boundaries of the White Sands National Monument are relatively safe because their fur is white. Meanwhile, some forty miles distant where the soil is dark because it consists of eroded black lava, other pocket mice also enjoy protective coloring—their dark brown or black fur makes them inconspicuous.

While the soft-furred desert pocket mouse *(Perognathus penicillatus)* has long hindlegs that help support it while digging with the forefeet, in most species both pairs of legs are the same length. Spiny pocket mice have a spoon-shaped claw on the hindfeet. It is used for grooming the fur and as a shovel.

Pocket mice are solitary creatures and live in individual burrows except during the breeding season. Some species merely excavate a straight tunnel in soft dirt which ends in a chamber in which they build a grass-lined nest. Other pocket mice construct a system of subways which run from the nest chamber to several storerooms. All pocket mice block the entrances to their burrows with dirt when they are at home. Spiny pocket mice also "close the door" when they leave their burrows.

During the day pocket mice remain in their burrows, hidden from enemies and shielded from the heat of the sun. At dusk they venture forth to forage for food, unless it is cold or raining. As indicated, pocket mice strip seeds from plants deftly and quickly, the forepaws packing the pouches so rapidly that the motion cannot be followed by the human eye.

Besides being outstanding harvesters, pocket mice are first-rate gleaners, sifting sand and dirt through the long claws on the forefeet, picking out any seeds, and putting them in their

Some pocket mice have limited ranges. Among these is Perognathus inornatus, *commonly known as the San Joaquin pocket mouse because it lives in California's San Joaquin Valley.*

pouches. About daybreak, when their pouches are full, the mice return home to feed and add any surplus to their caches in the storerooms. After emptying their pouches, the mice clean them by using special muscles that turn the pouches inside out and then pull them back into place.

Forest pocket mice enjoy a more varied menu than the pocket mice that live in deserts and other dry areas. They dine on leaves, nuts, and twigs as well as seeds. Incidentally, all species of pocket mice enjoy a meal in a cultivated field or in a granary. Pocket mice may also nibble an insect now and then. But they rarely if ever take a drink of water. Pocket mice have the ability to manufacture water from the plant material they eat.

While both spiny pocket mice and forest pocket mice breed throughout the year, silky pocket mice raise no families during the hot summer months. Females of all species usually have only two litters a year. The number of pups is normally four or five but may be as many as eight.

Pocket mice babies are born furred. The fur, irrespective of species, is soft and fine. The stiff, sharp bristles characteristic of the spiny pocket mice do not appear until the youngsters shed their baby fur when two months old and put on their adult pelage.

6. Fascinating Mice

"I will tell thee wonders."—Shakespeare

Field observation and laboratory research have revealed hundreds of fascinating facts about mice. For example, we have learned that the desert-dwelling cactus mouse *(Peromyscus eremicus)* passes the summer in a torpor in order to reduce its need for water. Zoologists have also discovered that the golden mouse *(Ochrotomys nuttalli)*, unlike most mice, is highly gregarious and shares its nest with others of the same species. Study of the spiny mouse of the Near East *(Acomys cahirinus)* has disclosed that it usually escapes if a predator seizes its tail, which is studded with stiff ridged spikes. But it is not the spikes that provide protection—the tail is extremely brittle and breaks off easily, while the mouse escapes. Meanwhile, Australian naturalists seek specimens of the dibbler *(Antechinus apicalis)*, one of the rarest of mammals. Like kangaroos, this marsupial mouse carries its young in a pouch.

Obviously, no book the size of this one could possibly detail all the information that has been gathered about mice. Indeed, it would take dozens of pages merely to list the names of the species and subspecies of mice that have been identified. Here, however, are accounts of some mice whose behavior is particularly fascinating.

Jumping Mice

A number of mice hop or leap. As a result, they are commonly but incorrectly called "kangaroo mice." Jumping mice—sometimes referred to as hopping mice—have a wide but spotty distribution. They are found in Australia's arid deserts, around the Caspian Sea, in the Chinese Province of Szechawn, and in eastern Siberia. There are also three species native to North America. Not only do these three species of mice closely resemble one another but also they can be distinguished from other jumping

Like the long hind legs and feet of kangaroos, those of jumping mice are specially modified for leaping. While airborne, Zapus hudsonius *and its relatives use their long, extremely thin tails as a balance.*

mice only by an examination of their teeth. North American jumping mice have fewer teeth than their foreign relations.

The description of the woodland jumping mouse *(Napaeozapus insignis)* that follows applies to the other two species of North American jumping mice in all respects except one—the woodland jumping mouse's tail is tipped with white. The tails of its relatives lack conspicuous coloration.

Insignis weighs less than an ounce. Its three- to four-inch body is covered—save for the white underparts—with a coat of rusty brown fur that is highlighted by a darker brown stripe along the back from nose to tail. The tail itself is extremely thin and often exceeds six inches in length. While jumping, the tail is used as a counterbalance which enables the mouse to make sharp turns in midair. If the tail is lost by accident, a jumping mouse is unable to keep its balance during a leap.

As is to be expected, the long hind legs and feet are specially adapted for jumping. The woodland jumping mouse is the most accomplished jumper for its size of all mammals. When pursued by an enemy, it can clear ten to twelve feet in a single bound. For a man to jump as far for his weight, he would have to leap four miles!

Jumping mice are rarely seen. Not only are they few in numbers but also they are nocturnal feeders. Their menu is a long and varied one. It includes berries, fruits, insects, meat, and dead fish. However, the staple food of jumping mice consists of grass seeds of all types. These are gathered in two ways. The mice either cut the stems of plants so that the seeds fall to the ground or bring the seeds within reach by climbing up stems which bend beneath their weight.

Spherical nests about eight inches in diameter made from dried vegetation serve jumping mice as summer homes. The nests may be hidden in a tussock of grass or other rank growth or suspended in a bush. If possible, nests are constructed near

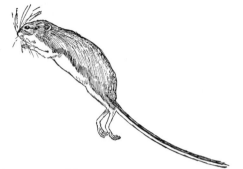

If a man could jump as far for his weight as a jumping mouse does, he would soar for four miles.

water. Jumping mice are outstanding swimmers.

Unlike most other mice, jumping mice hibernate. In late fall they retire to underground dens some three feet below the surface. In the oval chamber that they have filled with soft material, they roll in tight balls, curl their tails tightly around them, and sleep soundly until the arrival of spring.

Jumping mice mate twice a year. The first mating takes place in late March or early April, the second in midsummer. Each litter consists of three to six tiny, blind, naked, helpless babies. Within two weeks, the pups's bodies are almost completely furred and, a week later, their eyes open. When six weeks old, offspring cannot be distinguished from their parents and they leave the nest to make homes of their own.

Deer Mice

Mice sing. Their musical twitterings and chirping, which can be heard fifty feet away, are birdlike in quality. Dissection has disclosed that house mice that sing vocalize because they suffer from asthma, bronchial disorders, or a diseased larynx or lungs. But neither malformities nor disease is responsible for the music produced by certain white-footed mice that are commonly called deer mice. The most accomplished of these singers is the long-

Deer mice of the genus Peromyscus *are the North American equivalents of the wood mice of Europe. Among the species inhabiting open spaces is the prairie deer mouse shown here.*

tailed deer mouse *Peromyscus maniculatus.* During its nightly search for food, this mouse emits a high-pitched trill or "changes its tune" by sending out a prolonged buzzing. *Maniculatus* is also an outstanding drummer. When excited, it rapidly taps its front feet on the ground.

The long-tailed deer mouse along with the other species of white-footed mice that comprise the genus *Peromyscus* are the New World equivalent of the wood mice of Europe. Like their European counterparts, white-footed mice range far and wide. One species or another of white-footed mice is found from the Arctic Circle to Central America. Although the majority of white-footed mice are forest dwellers, a goodly number of species inhabit both swampy and dry areas.

No white-footed, white-bellied mouse is more agile than the woodland deer mouse. Like other members of the genus Peromyscus, *it is a most attractive and graceful creature.*

Only naturalists take the pains to differentiate between the various species of white-footed mice and call each by its proper name. Laymen are not so particular. This explains why the deer mouse has alternative names in different regions. In some areas it is known as the vesper mouse because it comes out of its nest at dusk and sings as a vesper sparrow does. Elsewhere the deer mouse is called the wood mouse because it lives in forests. The popular name deer mouse is derived from the color of the fur, which is reddish-brown like the fur of a deer.

However, the soft pelage of some white-footed mice is sandy buff. That of other species is dark brown, gray, or nearly black.

66

Still others are almost white. Immature individuals often have much darker fur than adults.

The color of their fur provides certain species of deer mice with a measure of protection from predators. Generally speaking, those deer mice that inhabit woodlands have dark fur while the fur of species living in open country or in arid areas is apt to be a light hue.

Most deer mice are medium sized. The hairy tail—which is usually as long as the head and the body combined—ranges from an inch and a half to eight inches in length.

Deer mice establish territories but do not defend them zealously. Even if the territories of two mice overlap—as they often do—fights are rare unless the area close to the nest is invaded. Research has established that not only are deer mice familiar with every inch of their home range but also they have a powerful homing instinct. In one experiment, captured deer mice were released two miles from their home ranges and found their way back to their nests without difficulty.

There may be several nests within the limits of a mouse's territory. Each nest is used only for a brief period. This is because deer mice are slovenly housekeepers. However, they do spend hours washing and grooming their fur.

Deer mice are not fussy about the location of their crude nests, fashioned from coarse vegetation and lined with moss, feathers, and fine grass. While deer mice may dig burrows to shelter their nests, they are more apt to construct them in the abandoned burrows of other small rodents, vacated bird and squirrel nests, under logs, or in hollow trees. They may move into summer cottages when the owners close them in the autumn and nest in drawers, stuffed furniture, or mattresses.

Nuts and seeds are the staple foods of deer mice. While not so destructive as meadow mice, deer mice cause considerable damage, particularly to newly planted crops. On the other hand,

Baby deer mice cling to their mother as she abandons a nest site.

they also eat a long list of harmful insects, as well as slugs, snails, and carrion. Thus these mice are both friends and foes of man.

Several different species of deer mice may inhabit the same area. This is proof that deer mice do not interbreed. Otherwise, the variations between the species would vanish. Zoologists have determined that the reason why the species do not mix is that each of them has a characteristic odor that enables the mice to distinguish members of their own species from those of other species.

Male deer mice seek mates with the approach of spring. Because of the overlapping of territories, they do not have to go very far. But finding potential mates is far easier than winning their affections. Eventually, however, the coy females accept their suitors and welcome them into their nests. The alliances usually last only a few days. However, research has revealed that, in some species of deer mice, the bond between male and female is long lasting.

Three to four weeks after mating, females produce one to nine blind, deaf, whiskered, naked babies. The youngsters cling so tightly to their mother's teats that she walks around dragging them beneath her. Deer mice are solicitous parents. When danger threatens, they haul their babies to a safe place—any that lose their grip and fall off are picked up by the back of the neck in the same fashion as a cat carries her kittens.

When two weeks old, the babies open their eyes. Now their development is rapid and they soon mature. Females begin breeding when seven weeks old and have four to five litters a year, each litter being raised in a new nest.

Normally, the breeding season of deer mice extends from spring to autumn, the fewest litters being produced during the summer. Breeding also will take place during mild winters.

Climbing Mice

Nearly every family includes an individual whose habits differ greatly from those of its kin. The genus *Phenacomys*—a group of four species of rare and little-known mice that resemble meadow mice in size and general appearance—has such a member. This noncomformist is the red tree mouse *(Phenacomys longicaudus)*. It lives in fir and spruce trees, feeding on the bark and the fleshy portions of the needles. The other three species are ground-dwelling seed and grass eaters.

A famine probably spurred *longicaudus* to climb trees in hopes

Despite the fact that the red tree mouse inhabits a small area and the widespread knowledge of this species' habits, Phenacomys longicaudus *has eluded photographers. As a result, this picture of a red tree mouse nibbling at needles is one of the rarest photographs of a mammal ever taken.*

of finding something to eat. Over the years, the species gradually became so dependent upon coniferous trees for food that it became a permanent resident of the treetops.

Not only does the long, loose-fitting, red-yellow coat of *longicaudus* distinguish it from the meadow mice to which it shows strong similarities but also from other members of the genus *Phenacomys*. All of *longicaudus'* kin have grayish-brown soft fur and short tails.

About half of the blunt-nosed, stocky red tree mouse's seven-inch length consists of a long, dark, hair-covered tail. This is why zoologists called the species *longicaudus,* which may be freely translated "long tailed."

High above the ground in the forests of northern California and Oregon, a red tree mouse may be born, grow to maturity, raise a family, and die without ever setting foot on soil. However, individual mice may, from time to time, climb down to the base of their "castle in the clouds."

When the sun is shining, tree mice move slowly along boughs, but they are swift and sure nocturnal climbers. Usually, they spend the daylight hours in their spherical nests which vary greatly in size but are always slightly flattened on the top.

Some nests are one hundred feet in the air and are so located that their owners can easily reach the branches of neighboring trees. Other nests are built thirty feet from the ground. Still others are constructed in the lower limbs of short saplings.

Often the highest nests are the deserted residences of gray squirrels which the mice have remodeled. Besides adding to the bulk of an abandoned nest when they move in, female red tree mice also tunnel a system of passageways through them. These passageways lead from the boughs on which the nest rests to a series of chambers. If a nest surrounds a trunk, the nest is pierced with a circular tunnel and the passageways fan out from it.

Tunnels also penetrate new nests which are fashioned from small twigs, lichens, stripped shoots, and excrement. Both old and new nests range in size from ovals a few inches in diameter erected on the end of a limb to huge structures a yard long and two feet high. Large nests are built close to the trunk and frequently encircle it, being supported by several thick boughs.

Even the largest of nests shelters but one female. Male tree mice also live alone for most of the year. Their small nests are usually located at the end of a limb.

As indicated, red tree mice are not numerous. This is due to several factors—their dependence on Douglas firs and Sitka spruce which limits their range, the toll taken by owls and other nocturnal predators, and the species' slow rate of reproduction. *Longicaudus* is not prolific, breeding but twice a year, in February and July. There are only one to four babies in a litter. Slow to mature, the babies do not leave their mother until they are a month old.

7. Laboratory Mice

"Science is nothing but perception."—Plato

Agriculturists, food processors, housewives, lumbermen, and manufacturers are constantly baiting traps and spreading poisons in hopes of killing as many mice as possible. Meanwhile, scientists rear millions of mice in their laboratories every year. Were it not for these mice, much of current biological investigation would be impossible.

Mice are indispensable in medical research for two reasons—they are short lived and they breed at a very early age. Thus researchers are able to determine the effects of experiments on a mouse throughout its entire life. Moreover, within a relatively short time, the impact of the same experiments on the mouse's immediate offspring and on many generations of its descendants can be established.

Man no longer believes in the Fountain of Youth or in a magic elixir whose properties could make the old young. But there never has been a greater interest in the causes of aging than at the present time. Researchers are convinced that once they discover how and why humans age they will be able to slow

The mouse on the right is named "Diabetes" for the disease it has. At left is its littermate, normal because it does not carry the mutated gene that causes diabetes.

Scientists engaged in medical research raise mutants—animals that differ from their parents. Here are three mouse mutants: clockwise from the top, piebald, with spotted coat; diabetes, with a condition similar to the human disease; and albino, with a white or nonpigmented coat.

down the aging process and improve the health of the elderly. The study of aging is called gerontology, a word derived from the Greek *geron* (old man).

Gerontologists—scientists engaged in the study of aging—use "inbred mice" in their experiments. A strain of inbred mice is developed by first mating brother and sister mice, then mating a brother and sister from their offspring. This process is repeated over and over. Eventually, all members of a strain have the

By selective breeding in the laboratory, scientists have developed mice with variegated fur. One of the most attractive of these strains is the piebald.

same characteristics—they are alike as identical twins. Some inbred strains are physically perfect. Others have malformities or are infected with disease. Still others suffer from malnutrition or are overweight.

After raising strains of inbred mice that differ from other

strains in one or more ways, scientists subject the various strains to exactly the same treatment. By carefully evaluating and recording the reactions of each strain they are able to gather data on how diet can shorten or lengthen life, determine the effects of radiation on the aging process, learn much about inheritance, and discover how the rate of growth and development can be speeded up or slowed down. Mice are also helping scientists learn how aging affects various organs in the human body. To gather information, the scientists transplant tissues from old mice into young mice and place tissues from young mice in old mice.

The human body is composed of many different kinds of cells. Most of these cells are constantly dividing. This division is the reason children grow, and why cuts, broken bones, and other injuries to the body heal. However, at times, the body produces unneeded cells. These, in turn, divide into more and more cells. One result of this uncontrolled growth is cancer—a leading cause of death.

In order to identify the agents that cause cancer and to determine how they stimulate normal cells to produce cancerous cells, scientists work with inbred mice. The mice are either exposed to materials thought to cause cancer, receive them in their food, have the materials smeared on their skin, or are injected with them.

Experiments with mice have established that certain viruses cause cancer in animals. This discovery has led researchers to investigate the possibility that some types of human cancers are also caused by viruses. Meanwhile, the increasing use of atomic reactors to generate electricity has motivated studies of the relationship between radiation and cancer. Mice are vital to this research, as they are to the experiments designed to determine whether or not cancer is inherited. Incidentally, mice have long been used as control animals in research into the causes of various diseases, the seeking of methods to prevent the spread of epidemics, and the search for cures.

Female house mouse with young. These animals are members of a strain that has been inbred at the world-famous Jackson Laboratory for about fifty years.

Because the pop-eyed, big-eared, long-tailed field mouse delights in nocturnal banquets of bulbs, beets, peas, and strawberries, it is the foe of gardeners throughout Asia, Europe, and North Africa. Extremely agile—it can jump as much as three feet when surprised—this long-tailed Old World field mouse does not hesitate to forage where there is no vegetation to conceal it from predators.

Let us hope that if inbred mice enable scientists to increase the human life span, find a cure for cancer, stamp out the diseases that presently plague mankind, and learn all the secrets of the hereditary mechanism, the age-old attitude toward mice will undergo a change. How about you? If a house mouse should take up residence in your attic and cause damage, or a field mouse destroy your garden, would you forget the contributions of laboratory-raised mice to mankind?

INDEX

Aesop, 24–25, 26
Africa, 11, 33
"Ancient mice," 12
Apollo, 17
Asia, 15, 16, 17, 33
Australia, 15, 62

Bali, 18
Barbary mouse, 14
Beach mouse, 47
Bible, 18
Bohemia, 21
Burns, Robert, 26

Cactus mouse, 61
Climbing mice
  appearance, 70–71
  behavior, 71
  mating, 71
  range and habitats, 71
  species, 69
Cricetids, 12
Czechoslovakia, 71

Deer mice
  appearance, 66–67
  food, 67–68
  habitat and range, 65
  homing instinct, 67
  mating, 69
  nests, 67
  singing, 64–65
Desert pocket mouse, 58
Dibbler, see Marsupial mouse
Dracula, 19

Eastern harvest mouse, 51
Europe, 33
European harvest mouse, 55

Field mice
  appearance, 41–42
  behavior, 42–44
  devastation by, 42
  distribution, 41
  enemies, 45
  mating, 44–45
  numbers, 41, 45
Forest pocket mouse, 56, 59, 60

Golden mouse, 61
Grasshopper mice
  appearance, 48
  behavior, 48–51
  food, 47–48
  mating, 51
  nests, 50
  species, 47
Greeks, 21

Harvest mice
  appearance, 53
  behavior, 53, 55
  food, 51
  mating, 55–56
  nests, 55
  range, 51
  species, 51
House mice
  appearance, 34
  behavior, 36, 38

House mice *(Continued)*
  damage by, 33
  enemies, 36
  mating, 38
  origin, 33
  range and habitats, 33–34
  vision and hearing, 34–35
Hystricomorphs, 10

"Inbred mice," 75–76

Japan, 33
Jews, 17, 18, 21
Jumping mice
  appearance, 63
  food, 63
  hibernation, 64
  mating, 66
  nests, 63
  range, 62
  species, 62–63

Laboratory mice, 7, 73, 75–76
Long-tailed deer mouse, 64–65

Marsupial mouse, 61
Meadow mouse, 41–45
Mice
  ancestry of, 10–11
  in art, 29
  in common speech, 30–31
  destruction by, 7, 33, 38–39, 67
  distribution of, 13, 15
  in literature, 24–27
  in medicine, 21–24
  music featuring, 30
  physical characteristics of, 13–14
  proverbs concerning, 7–28
  in religion, 17–19
  superstitions about, 16–21
Mickey Mouse, 29
Minnie Mouse, 29
"Modern mice," 12
Moore, Clement, 26
Mouse, popular definition, 12–13
Murids, 12
Myomorphs, 10, 11

New World mice, 12–13, 33, 62
Northern grasshopper mouse, 47 ff

Old Testament, 17
Old World mice, 12, 13–14
Orient, 11

Panchatantra, 24
Pine mouse, 47
Pliny the Elder, 21–22
Pocket mice
  appearance, 57–58
  food gathering, 58–59
  mating, 60
  nest, 58
  source of name, 56
  species, 50
Poulson, Emilie, 27
Protective coloring, 58, 67

Rats, 11, 33, 41
Red tree mouse, 89–92
Rodentia, 7–8, 10

Saint Kilda, 38
Sciuromorphs, 10
"Scorpion mouse," 47
Sethes, 29
Shakespeare, 26
Siberia, 62
Silky pocket mouse, 56, 57
South America, 11
Southern grasshopper mouse, 47 ff
Spiny mouse, 61
Spiny pocket mouse, 56–57, 60
Szechawn, 62

The Nutcracker, 30
Teeth, 8, 10
Transylvania, 19
Troy, 17
Tschaikovsky, 30

Vesper mouse, 66
Voles, 41
"Vole year," 45

"Waltzing mice," 36
Western harvest mouse, 51
White-footed mice, 65–66
Woodland jumping mouse, 63
Wood mouse, 60